The Story of Annie's Cradle Songs

GW00492653

By

SarahA O'Leary

Shield Crest

© Copyright 2024 SarahA O'Leary

All rights reserved.

This book shall not, by way of trade or otherwise, be lent, re-sold, hired out, or otherwise circulated without the prior consent of the copyright holder or the publisher in any form of binding or cover other than that in which it is published and without a similar condition including this condition being imposed on the subsequent purchaser. The use of its contents in any other media is also subject to the same conditions.

ISBN: 978-1-915657-57-2

A CIP catalogue record for this book is available from the British Library

MMXXIV

Published by

ShieldCrest Publishing
Boston, Lincolnshire, PE20 3BT
England.
www.shieldcrest.co.uk

In memory of Keith (1952-2019) who understood

For Jessica ~ to understand

For Annie ~ who is now understandable

Cover Images by Laura Cosby

Note to reader ~

~ with words in-be-tween; are meant to be smaller, to reflect whispers of a heartbeat. Yours and mine. Them and theirs.

Everything can be read individually or collectively.

But it is up to you (reader) what you take from reading such.

Be it a raging Wind, a scorching Sun; or even perhaps an Echo from the wilderness.

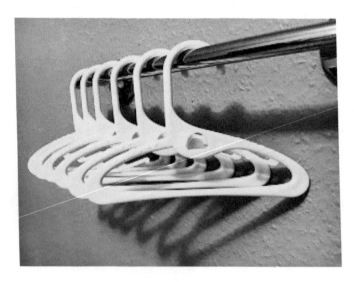

SarahA O'Leary

Contents

'The Story of Annie's Cradle Songs' 1

    'Tears of a Clown, Kept in a Fragile Vase' 2

    'An Embryo's Enigma' 3

    'Inner Child' 4

    'Tubes Like Drains' 6

    'Fetus Fall' 7

    'Cold Skin' 8

    'Shattered Silence' 9

    'Annie's Analogue' 10

    '(Un)locking Doors' 11

    'Willow's Lost Birthday' 12

    'Cold faces trace truth' 14

    'Catharsis of a Cataract' 16

    'Unwelcoming Beauty' 17

    'Words' 18

    'Mutation of a Monogram' 19

Epilogue 20

    'Never-Ending Nihilism' 20

Synonym 21

'Letters from Annie' 22

'sleep(less)' 23

'you forget' 24

'divorcing the silence' 25

'suggestive conscious' 26

'yours' 27

'a tattered love note' 28

Postscript 29

'bodiless brains on stilts' 30

'How I Dream You' 31

Afterword 32

About the Author 33

Acknowledgments 34

'The Story of Annie's Cradle Songs'

This is a story (that needs to be told), more than a
hundred, thousand days old.
Born from a dream once dreamt
and
given life, from a breath, breathed
through times torturous tears.

'Tears of a Clown, Kept in a Fragile Vase'

On coat hangers
vacant bodies swing
and
a tiny voice
of a desolate woman
begins to sing
a cradle song
to her
 (long-ago)
aborted twin.

N.B. Abortion ~ the deliberate ending of a human pregnancy

the natural ending of a pregnancy before the fetus is able to survive on its own

Synonyms ~ termination

Miscarriage

'An Embryo's Enigma'

I am the size of a bean
(the broad bean)
grown in the soil of the garden,
I grow inside
the womb
of a Woman
and yet,
still I feel pain,
the pain
(when no one holds my name)
as poisonous fluid
fuses inside my brain
(waiting for life within to cease)
just another crease
on a torn turned page.

Just another broken spoke,
on the world's wheel.

Each season's reason. Each turning tide of time,

There is a persisting presence of what's not really here or there (but here, in there; within…)

'Inner Child'

Child of my Spring
preserving within
all that I need
in my life to survive.

Child of my Summer
born with a lace of inspiration
entwined in her hair,
she carries a rainbow
of thoughts in her pockets
to disperse into the sky
of my dreams.

Child of my Autumn
knows what's important
as she acknowledges
the wealth of torrid tears
over smiles in her eyes.

Child of my Winter
lost in a snowstorm
with no smiles in her eyes
to staunch the sorrows
of all the tomorrows,
that show a vacuum
within my Soul.

children of my life's breath

Thoughts and feelings ponder on (wandering/wondering), like a breeze through the trees on a stifling summer night. Frightened (and yet not) by the light of knowledge becoming brighter with each passing pressing moment.

'Tubes Like Drains'

How did I
feel your hands
without you even
touching me?

How did
your breath
consume my breath
without me
breathing you?

* Waves wash stone
grey clear
oceans roar divorces
the silence *

My eyes, your eyes
My ears, your ears
My smell, your smell
My touch, your touch
My language…

…you.

'Fetus Fall'

White elephants
grow in my dreams.

Their limbs
attached to
neglected time
where I grieve
in the private
sanctuary
of my heart
and

sing hymns
to those bones
never fully formed

(my dreams always clasping
white elephants)

Contradicting chasms; of feelings, of emptiness. With an empty that can never really be filled. Is this what it feels like to be part of a missing whole? Cold.

'Cold Skin'

When you died, I lost
a dream.
Winter came, stayed
(never left) and
an embryo couldn't find her way
to daylight's growth.

When you died, my life
stopped living and
hope was never (more than)
a word
on a blank page
in a blank face.

are your fingers numb?

And, however much I try, solace can't be found in soundless time.

The never-ending strive for chimes, that are impossible to ring rhymes in my life.

'Shattered Silence'

My words, your echo
where there's no shelter from your breath,
that haunts my living space.

You can talk to me,
you can even stalk me
(walking behind me, following in my footsteps).

You can even love me, from far distant lands;
but laughter will always weave
frozen laced tears.
through my hands.

smile on me

*warm my bones **

'Annie's Analogue'

You had no name
and yet,
were the same as
the me that runs
through I…
Do you still
sleep, when I close my eyes?
Do you still sing, when I sigh?
Will you die (again)
when my life's breath
breathes no more
and a door can no longer be

walked through

Haunting hollow echoes and breaths, that can hardly breath, unbelieving life's living. Believing deaths unbelief.

'(Un)locking Doors'

Your shadow still
follows my Soul.
Your heartbeat continues
to hear
my broken breaths.
But you know how
your footsteps falter, in empty echoes

*dead fish swim
your tongue in my mouth
time's eye searching for truth *

Will I ever leave
a memory
a dream
a snow-angel untouched.

can you?

*Until found in a stranger's smile.
Until discovered amidst the silent sounds of a lonely, bound shore.
A distant memory.
A hazy glow.
A known lost word, forever lost
Reaching for the unreachable. Just out of reach.
Obscuring, mind's optic, observation.*

11

'Willow's Lost Birthday'

There is a room
next to her heart,
that in the late afternoon
smells of Lavender.

In a place
where the sun starts
to disappear behind the clouds
and where
you can hear
a child's silent tear
fall;
because
she was never baptized
at all.
Not even given the name
Jasmine.

It is a room
that has no door,
nor even a window
and there is no other
way
of reaching the swings
that lie within
a phantom playground.

For invisible is the summer
that sleeps
with the thieves
of Winter's sleeves
and dreams of
    (a) Baby's Breath.

'*Cold faces trace truth*'

At times
I want to
return.
(Or even arrive) at that place.

Yet,
we are always
there anyway really.
(Aren't we?)

Where our distances
fall away behind shadows
and
where
your frozen breath
dissolves on my tongue

But,
What if

*one day *

time drinks truths meaning?

What will happen
to all this
dreaming?

I'll stop
wanting to return.
(Or even arrive).

Because
we were/are
never really
there/here
anyway.

*are we? *

And so, there is no end, where there is/was no beginning. Just a hazy, lazy muddle of muddled misconceptions, that *will* live on and on…and on. Do you (reader), understand? Can you put my words together like a jigsaw puzzle and make the whole picture, so I might understand too? For…

'Catharsis of a Cataract'

I will always remember
the child clearly
who used to play
with me
in my Mother's womb.

She had a dirty face
and
sang sad songs,
born in a time
too soon.

Her crying
can be heard
echoing
in the chambers
of my Soul's tomb

still

Always
In all ways.

Yet, the numbness of knowing the unknown is always, in all ways; a welcoming of...

'Unwelcoming Beauty'

Are you ever lonely?
Do you feel (only),
that every Poem (every word)
is written about you.

Do you wonder what
your skin feels like, to be touched?

How much your lips burn cold…
… without
and how
dead children,
always call your name
(in the stillness of the night)
are you ever lonely then?

I am

'Words'

Opening windows
in my Soul
letting birds
fly free
telling the Sea
to come home.

unheard (of) screams

Annie,

Yes Annie, always my Annie. There in the background of my wanting, wishing; needing. You are my words. The breath between each breathing space.

If my destiny is that my life will never be complete, or only be a half-whispered (un)truth, then maybe (just maybe) by carrying around this heavy heart (of mine); I'll always keep alive the memory of Annie * my imaginary friend * * my inner child * * my lost twin*

'Mutation of a Monogram'

If I am the light of
your life's death/death's life,
you are the shadows
that follow me
and then;
fold away (each second's minute)
at the end
of every hour's day.

If you are my
silence, then I am
your silent echoes
that reverberate within
my words' Soul

If I am your
breath, then you
will always be
my life breathing.

* In this whispered story *

Epilogue

'Never-Ending Nihilism'

The empty cradle
rocks
and
lightning lights
the room, where each
night, steals silent
tears.

Where a clock
ticks

*Tortured time *

Synonym

I hold the heart of a dead child, within my own. It's the only way I know how to keep it beating. It's the only way I know how to keep my words breathing. Even if somewhat ragged, self-inflicted, wounds.

The guilt of a Daisy's survival, whilst stranded in the Desert. A Desert perishing, while a Daisy blooms. Or does she?

'Letters from Annie'

'sleep(less)'

your dreams hold an ache
insomnia lights candles
congregated pain.
because…

'you forget'

you forgot
that i (once)
touched you.
that when you open your mouth

*now *

the moon and sun shines out
and
your words' breath breathes
under the touch

*of me *

you forget.

'divorcing the silence'

was it not enough
that i loved
you?

that i offered you my
moon and sun;
filling your nights and days,
with longings?

that i gave you yourself
in perfection,
and
a hundred, thousand years
later
learnt to disguise
the bruises?

*is it not enough? *

'*suggestive conscious*'

i see my Soul
reflected in your eyes.
i feel my breath
breathing through your skin,
i hear my voice,
in the tinnitus whispers
of your deafened ears.

*to name and own every emotion of yours *

'yours'

days unborn
living in your dreams.

times touches
lost amongst your tears

and

withering winter leaves
now carpet the ground

in your every sunless summer

'a tattered love note'

*just stand still and i'll
move around you.
don't say a word and i'll
be your breath.*

*then close your eyes
to disguise the days' lies,
so, a pearl of great worth
falls to the earth
(surrounding you).*

just lie still (now) and i'll move with(in) you

Postscript

'bodiless brains on stilts'

Rocking back and forth,
swaying to and fro,
humming lost cords of
guitar strings…
… while holding within

*a young child

  once forgotten, amongst

  borrowed summer dreams

  now dancing through

  the screams of

  a psychiatric ward *

With years passing and without a doubt, still...

'How I Dream You'

I dream you, still alive
(A hive of thoughts engulfs my mind, surround my
Heart).
and this is the Poem I want to give to you.

The Poem that tells you how
the Moon is now my friend
and knows the way to
keep you full of life.

But only when she bathes (naked) in the black velvet
Skies
and my eyes are

closed

Afterword

Many, many Moons ago (when our Mother was alive), I had a conversation with her. It was shortly after I had lost my hearing, through the removal of bilateral acoustic neuromas. I believed something was taken away from me and in return I was given something of far greater value. My Poems. I felt/feel them. Almost as if they were/are whispered in my Soul's ears and flow through me.

And you know what she told me? Whilst pregnant with me, she lost a lot of blood (a **LOT** of blood), but this was back in the 60s, in the Far East; where/when no scans or anything were available to determine the cause of such.

When I was born, I was a 'breech birth'. Too, twins run in our wider family.

So, can you see, Dear Reader, my truth? The belief of my Poems?

About the Author

A Profoundly Deaf Poet. A Writer. A Dreamer. A Believer and as some may say "a mad woman".

A self-confessed poor student at school SarahA first started writing after losing her hearing (through the removal of Bilateral Acoustic Neuromas/benign brain tumors) in her mid-twenties. She feels as if something was taken away from her and in return, she was given something of far greater value... her writings. She always says that they come to her, like orphans sitting on the doorstep of her heart, waiting to be let in.

Having been published in several poetry magazines and anthologies, as well as previously self-publishing two poetry books; this is SarahA's first book where the publishers have taken a leap of faith in her, independent of her financial contribution.

Acknowledgments

Of course, my heartfelt thanks go firstly to my publishers for (as I stated previously) taking a leap of faith in me/my words/my story.

For MD: because even though you read such while still raw, you were blown away and then some. Helping me to believe in my story again.

For T(Dawn)S: after all these years I turned to you and it was never about me trusting you, but rather *you* still trusting me/my words.

And for My Family; past, present and future. For nurturing my heart and helping my words to breathe.

Sarah A O'Leary